What animal jump higher t house?

LOTS OF THEM CAN, A HOUSE CAN'T JUMP.

What's the best way to kill a circus?

Go for the juggler.

What do you call a cow with no legs?

Ground Beef.

"Ask me if I'm a truck."

"Are you a truck?"

"No."

Two cows are in a field chewing on grass. One turns to the other and says "Moo".

The other looks back and says "You bastard, I was about to say that."

Why'd the scarecrow win the Nobel prize?

He was outstanding in his field.

What shoes do ninjas wear?

Sneakers!

What did batman say to robin before they got in the car?

Robin, get in the car.

A mushroom walks into a bar and the bartender says "We don't serve your kind in here."

The mushroom replies "Why not? I'm a funguy"

How do you wake Lady Gaga up?

Poker face

What's the fruit that can't run away and get married?

... A Cantaloupe.

What's brown and sticky?

A stick!

What's big, green, and fuzzy, and would kill you if it fell out of a tree?

A pool table.

What happens if you throw a pink elephant into a purple lake?

It gets wet.

What did the ocean say to the beach?

Nothing, it just waved.

What did one hat say to the other hat?

You stay here; I'll go on ahead!

What did the farmer say after he lost his plow horse?

Where's my plow horse?

I have started to invest in stocks.

Beef,Chicken, and Vegetable.

One day I hope to be a bouillonaire.

What did the left butt cheek say to the right butt cheek?

You crack me up!

What's red and bad for your teeth?

A brick.

Whats green and has wheels?

Grass, I lied about the wheels

What's white and can't climb a tree?

A Fridge.

My mom died when we couldn't remember her blood type. As she died, she kept telling us to "be positive," but it's hard without her."

You don't need a parachute to go skydiving. You need a parachute to go skydiving twice.

What is the worst combination of illnesses?

Alzheimer's and diarrhea. You're running but can't remember where.

I'll never forget my Grandfather's last words to me just before he died.

"Are you still holding the ladder?"

What did the elephant ask the naked man?

"How do you breathe out of that thing?"

My girlfriend's dog died, so I bought her another, identical one. She just screamed at me and said:

"What am I meant to do with two dead dogs?!?"

My uncle named his dogs Timex and Rolex.

They're his watch dogs.

What do you call a useless piece of skin on a penis?

A man.

I tried to organize a professional hide-and-seek tournament, but it was a complete failure.

Good players are hard to find.

The guy that invented the umbrella was gonna call it the brella.

But he hesitated.

What do you call it when one cow spies on another?

A steak out!

I just went to an emotional wedding.

Even the cake was in tiers.

Why can't you hear a pterodactyl go to the bathroom?

Because the pee is silent.

SHIT

Did you hear about the two thieves who stole a calendar?

They each got six months.

I will never understand why manslaughter is illegal.

Men should be able to laugh at whatever they want.

Sometimes I tuck my knees into my chest and lean forward.

That's just how I roll.

I got fired from my job at the bank today. An old lady came in and asked me to check her balance, so I pushed her over.

SHIT

Why did the sperm cross the road?

Because I put on the wrong sock this morning.

What do you call it when Dwayne Johnson buys a cutting tool?

Rock pay-for scissors.

What do you call a pony with a sore throat?

A little horse.

I broke my arm in two places. You know what the doctor told me?

"Stay out of those places!"

Ever tried to eat a clock?

It's time-consuming.

What do you call a dog with no legs?

You can call him whatever you want, he's still not coming.

What do you call a boomerang that never comes back?

A stick.

Why did the invisible man turn down the job offer?

He couldn't see himself doing it.

What do you call birds who stick together?

Vel-crows.

Why can't a nose be 12 inches long?

Because then it'd be a foot.

What kind of music do mummies listen to?

Wrap music.

I hate Russian dolls.

They're so full of themselves.

What did the janitor say when he jumped out of the closet?

"Supplies!"

What do sprinters eat before a race?

Nothing, they fast.

I'm not a big fan of stairs. They're always up to something.

Did you hear the rumor about butter?

Never mind, I shouldn't spread it.

Did you know the first French fries weren't cooked in France?

They were cooked in Greece!

Did you see the documentary about beavers?

It was the best dam show I ever saw!

What did the little mountain say to the bigger mountain?

Hi Cliff!

What did one wall say to the other?

Meet me at the corner!

What do you call a pig that does karate?

A pork chop.

If you receive a picture of some meat in a tin from me to your email address...

don't worry, it's just spam.

Why don't dinosaurs talk?

Because they're dead

What do an apple and an orange have in common?

Neither one can drive.

Two cannibals are eating a clown. One says to the other, "Does this taste funny to you?"

You know, people say they pick their nose, but I feel like I was just born with mine.

Why was the math teacher late to work?

She took the rhombus.

My wife is really mad at the fact that I have no sense of direction. So I packed up my stuff and right.

I'm reading a book about anti-gravity.

It's impossible to put down.

How is a woman like a grenade?

Remove the ring and boom, the house is gone!

Does anyone need an ark?

I Noah guy.

I'm only familiar with 25 letters of the alphabet.

I don't know why.

What do you give a sick bird?

Tweetment.

Why did the picture go to jail?

Because it was framed!

What did the drummer call his two twin daughters?

Anna One, Anna Two.

What do you call a can opener that doesn't work?

A can't opener.

What's the No. 1 cause of divorce?

Marriage!

I bought sneakers from a drug dealer. I don't know what he laced them with but I've been tripping all day!

What shivers at the bottom of the ocean?

A nervous wreck.

What do you call someone who points out the obvious?

Someone who points out the obvious.

I sold my vacuum yesterday. It was just collecting dust.

Printed in Great Britain
by Amazon

33891075R00030